SUMMARY

An apparent lack of interest by Russia in Sub-Saharan Africa over recent years masks persistent key strategic drivers for Moscow to reestablish lost influence in the region. A preoccupation with more immediate foreign policy concerns has temporarily interrupted a process of Russia's reclaiming relationships, well-developed in the Soviet period, to secure access to mineral and energy resources that are crucial both to Russia's economic and industrial interests and to its existing and new markets for military arms contracts.

Russian policy priorities in Africa provide both challenges and opportunities for the U.S. in fields such as nuclear nonproliferation, as well as energy security for the United States and its European allies. These priorities indicate that Russian development of key resources in southern Africa should be observed closely. Russian trade with the region is significantly underdeveloped, with the exception of the arms trade, which Russia can be expected to defend vigorously if its markets are challenged, including by the prospect of regime change or international sanctions. At the same time, Russia and the United States have a shared interest in restricting the freedom of movement of terrorist organizations in ungoverned or lightly governed spaces in Africa, which opens potential for cooperation between U.S. Africa Command (AFRICOM) initiatives and Russian presence in the region.

Overall, Russian diplomatic and economic activity in southern Africa should receive continuing attention from U.S. policymakers due to its direct relevance to a number of U.S. strategic concerns.

i

RUSSIAN INTERESTS
IN SUB-SAHARAN AFRICA

INTRODUCTION

> What I therefore propose to do here is . . . to illustrate
> the most varied aspects of Russia's African policy
> down the centuries: alliances, colonisation projects,
> plans for protectorates, religious propaganda, naval
> demonstrations with the object of maintaining the
> status quo, and on the other hand, conspiracy and un-
> derground activity with a view to altering the political
> map of Africa. No less varied have been the motives
> which have over and over again brought Africa closer
> to the attention of Russia.
>
> Sergius Yakobson,
> *The Slavonic and East European Review*, 1939[1]

Twenty years after World War II, U.S. Secretary of
State Dean Acheson said that Great Britain had "lost
an empire and has not yet found a role." Twenty years
after the fall of the Soviet Union, the same can be argued of Russia. Since the dissolution of the Union of
Soviet Socialist Republics (USSR), the Russian Federation has been trying both to establish its place in the
world and to set formative policies in order to reassert
itself on the world stage as a major international power. More recently, Russian foreign policy has sought to
move from reactive to proactive policies to safeguard
interests abroad, while seeking to preserve this perceived global power status.

Sub-Saharan Africa is a key arena of contest for
global power influence in the coming decades due not
only to the region's disproportionately strong potential for economic growth in the near to medium term,[2]
but also and especially in order to ensure access to the

1

wealth of natural resources located there, an essential prerequisite for long-term development plans. But, while Russia, along with other powers, seeks to establish its interests in Sub-Saharan Africa, laying claim to and extracting these resources would require immense investment that, for Russia, could outweigh the potential gain in the near term. The Russian Federation seeks to establish a presence in Africa, and more than presence, influence; but some of Russia's efforts in this direction can be interpreted as a placeholder or stopgap until Russia establishes a coherent overarching policy toward the region. In the meantime, Russian businesses and investors are cherry-picking resources and investing on a strictly commercial basis in sub-Saharan Africa.

In this monograph, the author will assess the resurgent Russian desire to seek economic opportunities in Sub-Saharan states, the recent implementation of this aim, and overall Russian objectives in the region. The extent of penetration of Russian influence in the area relative to other powers such as China and the United States will be assessed, and the potential implications for U.S. interests in the region considered.

HISTORY

As illustrated by the quotation at the beginning of this monograph, Russian interests in, and ambitions for, Africa have been many and varied over a period dating back to Tsarist times. For the purpose of considering Russia's current engagement with the region, we need to consider antecedents in the late Soviet period, as relations and attitudes established then still govern some aspects of engagement today. The relevant period begins following the death of

2

Josef Stalin in 1953. Until this point, relations between the USSR and African states had been insignificant, as African states controlled by the colonial powers were considered by the USSR to be a part of the capitalist system and unsuitable for penetration by Soviet influence. But the change of power in the Soviet Union from Stalin to Nikita Khrushchev coincided with the burgeoning of independence movements in Africa, triggering Soviet interest in the possibilities offered by engagement with newly-independent states and anti-colonial movements across the continent. As one historical study notes:

> In 1955, the Soviet Union made its first major arms transfer to an African country, Egypt. Within 10 years, the Soviets had established diplomatic ties with newly-independent Algeria, Ghana, Guinea, Mali, Sudan, Morocco, and Libya. These Soviet allies, referred to as the "Casablanca Bloc" after they had held their first summit in Casablanca, Morocco, were invited to attend the Twenty-Second Congress of the Communist Party of the Soviet Union (CPSU) in Moscow in 1961.[3]

A key aim of this Congress in 1961 was to outline the vision expressed by Soviet leader Khrushchev of how developing African countries could bypass capitalism and advance straight to socialism, fostered by the USSR. As with later efforts in Afghanistan, this Soviet doctrinal standpoint failed to take into account local realities: social disorder, domestic rivalry, and political instability, which derailed attempts to attain socialist paradise in two easy steps. Attempts to incite revolution in a number of states notionally friendly toward the USSR damaged Soviet credibility.[4] Counter-coups overthrowing pro-Soviet leaders in Algeria (1965), Ghana (1966), and Mali (1968) led Soviet analysts to acknowledge that their initial goals for Africa had been unrealistic.[5]

Following the late 1960s, Soviet policy goals shifted. Economic relations with some African countries were now aimed at commercial benefits without ideological riders, while maintaining the aim of furthering Soviet global influence. Simultaneously, Soviet sponsorship of military and terrorist confrontation with, first the colonial powers, and later, Rhodesia and South Africa, absorbed considerable Soviet resources. Following the Portuguese revolution in 1974, which gave Communist countries freedom of operation in the newly, and unexpectedly, independent Angola and Mozambique, the extent of Soviet-backed support for terrorist and guerrilla operations against Rhodesia was such that a border area opposite Mozambique ironically became known among Rhodesian forces as "the Russian Front."[6] Support on this scale throughout Africa was not without direct risk, and casualties were suffered, although never avowed at the time—as, in one example, when 11 Soviet secret police (KGB) officers were captured and shortly afterwards shot during an insurgent attack on President Kwame Nkrumah's residence in Accra, Ghana, in 1966.[7]

The Cold War period saw investments of funds, manpower, and materiel by the USSR and its allies that are at least comparable with U.S. and coalition activities overseas today—as is demonstrated by the Cuban effort in Angola, which peaked at an estimated 30,000 "advisers" in 1982.[8] As well as sponsoring troop and equipment contributions by allies, the USSR also directly supplied substantial contingents of KGB and military advisers throughout southern Africa.[9] This constituted the main source of support and assistance for independence movements in many African countries, not least to the banned African National Congress (ANC) and its military wing, Umkhonto we Sizwe, seeking to subvert authority in South Africa. This contribution, coupled with the fact that many African leaders personally received education and support from the USSR, created a generally positive, anti-colonialist image of Russia in the region.[10] At the same time, in a curious parallel, Russian ex-KGB and ex-military "combat comrades" who served together in Angola and elsewhere in Southern Africa formed a coherent mutual support group that needs to be considered when examining Russian elite politics[11] and may provide a partial explanation for the apparently disproportionate focus of Russian economic interests in Angola when compared to other states in the region.

In a precursor of today's competition for influence in Africa between the Russian Federation and China, to be discussed in more detail below, there was a division of labor, and sometimes even competition, between the USSR and China on sponsoring revolutionary movements and arming client states. Temporary relative dominance by the USSR on the continent followed the pattern of Soviet decline and resurgence of interest in the region during the Cold War[12] — again, a pattern repeated more recently with the Russian withdrawal from engagement with Africa seen immediately following the demise of the USSR in 1991, also to be discussed further below.

Although support for revolutionary and terrorist movements was the most evident form of Soviet engagement in Africa during the Cold War, this support was not to the exclusion of pursuing other interests, particularly economic ones. South Africa in particular became both a locus of ideological confrontation and a fertile ground for technical espionage in the 1980s.[13] South Africa's rich resource base and direct competition with the USSR, in diamond mining in particular, led to a strange ambivalence in bilateral relations. At the same time as it was providing substantial and direct ongoing support for the ANC and Umkhonto we Sizwe,[14] the USSR was engaging in covert cooperation with the South African government, which each of these groups was striving to overthrow. According to Christopher Andrew and Vasiliy Mitrokhin:

> There were deep contradictions at the heart of Soviet policy towards southern Africa. Despite its uncompromising denunciation of apartheid, Moscow maintained top-secret contacts with Pretoria over the regulation of the world market in gold, diamonds, platinum and precious metals, in which the Soviet Union and South Africa between them had something of a duopoly. Because of the extreme sensitivity of these contacts and the outrage which their public disclosure would provoke in black Africa, the KGB took a prominent part in arranging them. . . . In the mid-1980s, De Beers Corporation in South Africa was paying the Soviet Union almost a billion dollars a year for the supply of high quality diamonds. Moscow's lucrative secret arrangements with Pretoria to keep mineral prices high did not prevent it attacking South Africa's Western business partners for doing business with apartheid.[15]

Out of Africa.

The years immediately following the collapse of the Soviet Union in 1991 saw a dramatic reduction in Russia's involvement in Africa. The legacy of Soviet involvement, and the state of bilateral relations between the USSR and African nations at the end of the Soviet period, was, in effect, put on ice.

The foreign policy of the new, "independent" Russian Federation changed drastically, as the state focused on reorganizing at home, facing new challenges, and struggling to find a place in the post-Cold War world. Preoccupied with managing dangerous domestic chaos, the new government could not formulate a coherent Africa policy and signaled a retreat from relations with Africa by closing nine embassies, three consulates, and multiple cultural centers[16] while at the same time exchanging bitter recriminations over the prospects for recovery of the huge debt owed to the Soviet Union by African states. Amid deep financial crisis, then-President Boris Yeltsin ceased foreign aid and persisted in requests for African governments to repay the Soviet loans, despite pleas by those governments for reductions or other deferred payment options. Russia's reversal in policy left a number of African governments feeling abandoned by Russia and presented a significant obstacle for Moscow to overcome when Russia eventually regained interest and sought to re-establish relations with Sub-Saharan Africa. In marked contrast, during precisely the same period, China greatly increased its profile throughout the continent, with the first wave of the huge Chinese investment there that has continued ever since.[17]

According to leading historian of Soviet involvement in Africa and Deputy Director of the Institute for African Studies at the Russian Academy of Sciences Vladimir Shubin, after December 1991 the Russian policy toward southern Africa was "largely determined by personalities or clans, acting either in their own narrow interests or blinkered by 're-ideologization', and certainly not in Russia's national interests."[18] This included switching allegiance from the ANC to the by now short-lived white minority government in South

Africa for, Shubin suggests, short-term commercial and often personal interests.[19] More recently, however, Russian officials and academics alike have been convinced that there are economic and pragmatic foreign policy advantages to re-engagement with Africa.

Return to Africa.

The hiatus in relations between Russia and Africa was replaced in the early 2000s by a determination to re-establish a presence in the region, spurred by concern that China, India, Brazil, and especially the United States were intensifying their involvement there in order to secure access to natural resources and energy reserves. Russian government officials were open and explicit as to the benefits of returning to Africa, while persistently repeating the theme of Russia's Soviet-era prominence and diligence in support to Africa to attempt to re-foster good relationships with African nations and rebuild trust. Then-Russian Foreign Minister Igor Ivanov noted in 2001 that

> Our country played the vanguard role in the de-colonization of Africa and helped several countries in their independence struggles. Today's African leaders remember that very well.[20]

Vladimir Putin's visit to the Republic of South Africa in 2006 was the first ever visit by a Russian leader to sub-Saharan Africa, and the highlight of a series of bilateral visits at ministerial levels and above with South Africa, Angola, and Ethiopia. This gave impetus to a wave of Russian investment by, according to the Russian Ministry of Foreign Affairs, confirming the presence of real opportunities for the Russian business community by relying on stable political contacts to make a breakthrough in the field of trade and economic cooperation.[21]

In June 2009, then-President Dmitry Medvedev, along with a delegation of 300 businessmen, took a highly publicized tour of the region including Nigeria, Angola, and Namibia. This further high-level visit was indicative of Moscow's intensifying desire to foster investment and involvement in the region by means of visible government sponsorship. Political initiatives included, with South Africa in particular, a Treaty of Friendship and Cooperation covering joint work in healthcare and intellectual property rights.[22] According to *Africa Economic Brief*, these visits and accompanying initiatives on conflict resolution, humanitarian assistance, and debt relief for Africa were an attempt to address Russia's marginal importance as a trading partner for African countries when compared to the European Union (EU), the United States, China, India, and Brazil. Although the volume of trade between Russia and Africa grew ten-fold between 1994 and 2008, this was from a minuscule starting point of just $740 million annually in the immediate post-Soviet period.[23]

The Russian interest in securing access to natural resources that are either unobtainable or depleted in Russia and in its traditional trading partners, explored in more detail below, throws into sharp focus the late and slow start Russia has made in this process when compared with China. Driven by a more urgent need to secure natural resources and availability of copious funding, the Chinese presence in the region intensified as Russia withdrew from Africa and now dwarfs that of Russia. Chinese involvement in Africa also includes a bilateral trade element largely missing in the case of Russia: China has, in addition, cultivated African economic markets, with African households purchasing $31 billion more in Chinese consumer goods than from Russia.[24] Russian media commentary agonizes over the growing influence of China in Africa, and in particular its prodigious funding,[25] but without offering constructive advice on whether this is a problem for Russia and, if so, what to do about it.[26] Yet Russian officials have continuously stated that increased economic and political engagement with Sub-Saharan Africa will be important to securing profitable and easily cultivated sources of natural resources.

RUSSIA'S PRESENCE TODAY— POLITICAL PRIORITIES

Russian political aspirations in Africa include regaining the leverage once enjoyed by the Soviet Union by re-establishing presence as well as by building new ties, especially since Medvedev's flagship 2009 visit. Russia's current strategy to achieve these aims appears built around the aim of achieving political gains at low financial cost. Talk is cheap, as indeed are promises, and with this in mind, Russian officials are endeavoring to keep a Russian presence in the forefront of African minds by means of consistent bilateral diplomatic meetings in order to pave the political roads for pragmatic, carefully selected economic involvement.

One of the methods Moscow uses in this attempt to regain influence is to keep Russia's Soviet involvement and role as a noncolonial power prominent in media reporting and in official Russian speeches on African relations. Russian politicians and academics assert that Russia never left Africa, nor were they ever a colonial power in Africa, maintaining this consistent discourse in order to pave the way for a smoother re-entry into influence on the continent. Moscow has stressed "ideology free" diplomacy during this process, indirectly countering the U.S. policy of stressing democracy and human rights, as well as insisting that African governments should battle against corruption. In 2001, Foreign Minister Ivanov referred to Russia in Africa as a "time tested and reliable ally,"[27] repeating that, unlike many other countries, Russia had assisted in decolonization and in achieving independence. Yet 8 years later, during his 2009 visit to Africa, Medvedev told the media: "Frankly, we were almost too late. We should have begun working with our African partners earlier."[28]

Several Russian officials and prominent academics have publicly stated that future relations with Africa will continue to ensure no signs of neocolonial ambition, thereby attempting to assuage African fears of Russian political intent in relations with Sub-Saharan Africa. There are limited attempts at exerting soft power in the region: as part of a global Russian aspiration to leverage the attraction of Russian language and culture, the "Russian Schools Abroad" cultural program plans to open "Russian centers of science and culture" in Mali, Algeria, Kenya, Guinea, and Sudan.[29] Direct aid programs are similarly limited: Russia's overall aid spending dropped from $785 million in 2009 to $472.32 million in 2010—a decrease of 40 percent. But according to a Russian Ministry of Finance report released in advance of the 2011 G8 summit in Deauville, France, this reflected a temporary decrease in Russia's aid budget in 2009 as a response to the global financial and economic crises, with the additional assistance particularly targeted at neighboring former Soviet republics.[30] Meanwhile, a key overture to pave the way for Russia's reinsertion into Africa was Moscow's eventual waiver of a number of African states' Soviet debts, estimated at $20 billion in 2009.[31] In 2009, the African Coordinating Committee for Economic Cooperation with African Countries (AfroCom) was created with the intention of fostering increased political and economic cooperation through an international business forum "designed to create a space for Russian and African businessmen and politicians to network." Moscow hosted the first Russian-African inter-parliamentary summit in June 2009, heralded by Deputy Chairman of AfroCom Petr Fradkov, as the "biggest political event of such extent in history of Russian-African relations."[32]

In purely political terms, Moscow's continuing foreign policy aim of asserting a multipolar international system will encourage it to seek to counter the unrestrained influence of global powers in Africa, especially the United States and China. Russia's key lever of power in international affairs, a veto in the United Nations Security Council (UNSC), could be expected to come into play if Moscow feels unable to achieve this aim by other means. Russia needs African nations, which compose nearly a quarter of the UN, to support Moscow-led initiatives in order for Russia to not appear isolated on the international stage and, instead, point to a degree of global support for Russia's political position. The political attraction of specific initiatives developed by Russia should not be underestimated: in the topical field of cyber security, for example, the Russian and Chinese proposals for regulation of the internet, which are trenchantly opposed by the Euro-Atlantic community, enjoy an often overlooked degree of support in Africa and elsewhere.

In return, Moscow supports African nations in the UNSC. In 2008, Russia voted against imposing sanctions and arms embargos on Robert Mugabe's Zimbabwe. Russian UN Ambassador Vitaliy Churkin stated that he did not vote to impose sanctions on Zimbabwe because there was no threat to international peace and security, and that the matter had not spread beyond being a purely domestic issue.[33] However, any mandate voted would have halted any Russian arms sales to Zimbabwe, cutting off future potential arms markets. In a similar vein, in August 2012, Russian Deputy Foreign Minister Mikhail Bogdanov and Special Presidential Envoy to the Middle East and Africa Mikhail Margelov traveled to Ethiopia, Liberia, Madagascar, Uganda, and Zimbabwe to encourage political support for Russia's position on the conflict in Syria—another key client for Russian arms sales.[34] Special Envoy Margelov in particular is an especially experienced Africa expert by Russian standards, gaining his first experience of Africa as a child accompanying his father, Vitaliy, on repeat postings there during the latter's KGB career.[35]

Russia also provides a limited amount of indirect support for the African Union (AU) through involvement in peacekeeping training and missions. As of 2010, Russia was participating in all UN peacekeeping missions in Africa and training 400 peacekeepers from Africa in Russia.[36] There is a clear Russian interest in maintenance of peace and regional stability in Africa in order to secure access to natural resources and protect investments, while at the same time paradoxically ensuring that African demand for Russian arms remains strong. However, according to UN statistics, in August 2012, Russia was contributing fewer than 100 police, servicemen, and experts overall to all

15 UN peacekeeping missions.[37] Despite professed support from Moscow for AU aims, in October 2011, Foreign Minister Sergei Lavrov stated that, while relations with the AU remain strong, bilateral cooperation offered more economic opportunity, emphasizing that Russia's trade turnover with African countries south of the Sahara is worth some $4 billion, while China enjoys a $120 billion turnover.[38] Lavrov also illustrated successful bilateral relations by highlighting African joint projects with Russia's Gazprom, RusAl, Renovo, Lukoil, and Alrosa companies, the most active Russian companies in Africa.

ECONOMIC AIMS

According to Vladimir Shubin, as Russia grows more confident in its foreign policy objectives, Russia and Africa "need each other" in order to ensure the security and sovereignty of 60 percent of the world's natural resources, which lie in Russia and Africa combined.[39] To this end, the tasks of the Asia and Africa department of Russia's Ministry of Economic Development include developing bilateral relations "in accordance with the priorities of the Foreign Economic Strategy of the Russian Federation to 2020."[40] The Africa section of these priorities, drawn up in 2008, is worth quoting, since it gives an intriguing overview of Russian strategic aims, while at the same time retaining the slight air of detachment from reality that habitually accompanies Russian strategic aspirations. Section 5.6 is quoted in detail as follows:

5.6. Countries of the Middle East and Africa.

The main goal of foreign policy in the region is building sustainable trade and investment relations with the leading countries of the Middle and Near East [note no mention of Africa] that can grow Russian exports, including of machinery and technical products. . . .

Africa, being a swiftly growing region, represents a strategic interest to the Russian economy, including as a source of natural resources, a market for investment projects and a market for exports of machinery and technical products exports. . . .

The priorities of the foreign economic strategy in the region are:

- Prospecting, mining, oil, construction and mining, purchasing gas, oil, uranium, and bauxite assets (Angola, Nigeria, Sudan, South Africa, Namibia, etc.);
- Construction of power facilities — hydroelectric power plants on the River Congo (Angola, Zambia, Namibia, and Equatorial Guinea) and nuclear power plants (South Africa and Nigeria);
- Creating a floating nuclear power plant, and South African participation in the international project to build a nuclear enrichment center in Russia;
- Railway Construction (Nigeria, Guinea, and Angola);
- Creation of Russian trade houses for the promotion and maintenance of Russian engineering products (Nigeria and South Africa).

As with the regions of the Middle East, an urgent task for Africa is the participation of Russian companies in the privatization of industrial assets, including those created with technical assistance from the former Soviet Union (Iran, Turkey, Morocco, Nigeria, Guinea, and Angola).[41]

RESOURCE INTERESTS—MINERALS

It is notable that the first priority shown in the list above concerns prospecting and mining and that, in terms of access to natural resources, Africa represents a "strategic interest" for Russia. According to forecasts, Russia's economically viable reserves of a number of minerals essential for the functioning of a modern economy, including zinc, manganese, copper, nickel, and platinum, will be depleted within a decade. Although Russia possesses significant untapped resource deposits, these are often difficult to access and costly to develop. For this reason, and given the volatility of world commodity prices, it is in the economic interests of Russia to gain access to sources of supply of such strategic minerals in regions where costs are lower, in particular in Southern Africa.[42] Table 1 shows the estimated depletion date for a range of minerals in Russia and their availability in Southern Africa, specifically the Southern African Development Community (SADC) nations,[43] in order to illustrate the extent of this complementarity.[44]

It is partly for this reason that Russian economic expansion into Africa has involved primarily those industries in which Russian companies have been most active and successful domestically in the post-Soviet period, namely extraction of ferrous and nonferrous metals, diamonds, and energy. Table 2 from a 2011 *Africa Economic Brief* lists major Russian investment projects in Africa.[45]

	Russia's Natural Resource Base Complementarities with Southern Africa			
Mineral	Year in which Russia will deplete		SADC countries that possess reserves of the mineral (in alphabetical order)	SADC share in the world's total resources of the mineral
	economically producible reserves	all reserves		
Lead	2007	Beyond 2025	Namibia / South Africa / Zambia	-
Manganese ores	2008	Beyond 2025	DRC / South Africa	83%
Zinc	2011	Beyond 2025	DRC / Namibia / Zambia	-
Chromium ores	2013	Beyond 2025	Madagascar / South Africa / Zimbabwe	93%
Diamonds	2013	Beyond 2025	Angola / Botswana / DRC / Lesotho / Namibia / South Africa / Tanzania	>50%
Quartz	2013	2013	Madagascar / Mozambique	-
Tin	2015	Beyond 2025	DRC / Namibia / South Africa / Tanzania / Zimbabwe	-
Uranium	2015	Beyond 2025	Angola / DRC / Namibia / South Africa / Zambia	12%

Table 1. Mineral Estimated Depletion Dates in Russia and Their Availability in Southern Africa.

Russia's Natural Resource Base Complementarities with Southern Africa				
Mineral	Year in which Russia will deplete		SADC countries that possess reserves of the mineral (in alphabetical order)	SADC share in the world's total resources of the mineral
	economically producible reserves	all reserves		
Gold	2015	Beyond 2025	Angola / DRC / Namibia / South Africa / Tanzania / Zambia / Zimbabwe	53%
Oil	2015	Beyond 2025	Angola / DRC	-
Copper	2016	Beyond 2025	Angola / Botswana / DRC / Namibia / South Africa / Zambia / Zimbabwe	8%
Nickel	2016	Beyond 2025	Botswana / South Africa / Tanzania / Zimbabwe	10%
Tungsten	2016	Beyond 2025	Namibia	-
Platinum-group metals	2018	Beyond 2025	South Africa / Zimbabwe	88%
Graphite	2018	Beyond 2025	Madagascar / Mozambique	-

Table 1. Mineral Estimated Depletion Dates in Russia and Their Availability in Southern Africa. Cont.

	Russia's Natural Resource Base Complementarities with Southern Africa			
Mineral	Year in which Russia will deplete		SADC countries that possess reserves of the mineral (in alphabetical order)	SADC share in the world's total resources of the mineral
	economically producible reserves	all reserves		
Coal	Beyond 2025	Beyond 2025	Botswana / DRC / Madagascar / South Africa / Swaziland / Tanzania / Zambia / Zimbabwe	12%
Phosphate	Beyond 2025	Beyond 2025	Angola / South Africa / Tanzania	10%
Potash	Beyond 2025	Beyond 2025	Botswana	-
Bauxite	Beyond 2025	Beyond 2025	Angola / Madagascar	-
Iron ores	Beyond 2025	Beyond 2025	Angola / Botswana / South Africa / Tanzania / Zimbabwe	5%
Natural gas	Beyond 2025	Beyond 2025	Angola / DRC / Mozambique / South Africa / Tanzania	-
Vanadium	Beyond 2025	Beyond 2025	South Africa	-
Fluorspar	Beyond 2025	Beyond 2025	Angola	-
Salt	Beyond 2025	Beyond 2025	Botswana / Madagascar / Namibia / South Africa	-

**Table 1. Mineral Estimated Depletion Dates
in Russia and Their Availability in Southern Africa. Cont.**

	Major Investments of Russian Companies in Africa				
Russian Investor	Host Country/ *Company*	Industry	Type of Investment	Value	Year
Norilsk Nickel	South Africa *Gold Fields*	Gold mining and processing	M&A (acquired 30% of Gold Fields)	$1.6 billion	2004
Norilsk Nickel	Botswana *Tati Nickel*	Nickel mining and processing	M&A (acquisition of Canada Lion Ore Mining gave it 85% stake in Tati Nickel)	$2.5 billion	2007
Sintez	South Africa, Namibia, Angola	Oil, gas, diamonds and copper exploration	Greenfield Investment	$10–50 million	2006
Lukoil	Côte d'Ivoire, Ghana	Oil exploration	M&A (acquired interest in 10,500 km² deep water blocks)	$900 million	2010
Rusal	Nigeria *ALSCON*	Aluminum refining	M&A (acquired majority stake in Aluminum Smelter Company - ALSCON of Nigeria)	$250 million	2008
Severstal	Liberia	Iron ore	M&A (acquired control of iron ore deposit in Putu Range area of Liberia)	$40 million	2008
Gazprom	Algeria *Sonatrach*	Natural gas exploration	Joint exploration and development projects by debt write-off agreement and arms deal	$4.7 billion and $7.5 billion	2006
Alrosa	Angola, Namibia, DRC	Diamond mining, and hydroelectricity	Greenfield Investment	$300–400 million	1992

Table 2. Major Russian Investments Projects in Africa.

A striking feature of this table is the early date for the major investment project listed for Angola. Angola was one of the Sub-Saharan African countries that enjoyed the most intense and the most recent attentions of the USSR, during the armed conflict there and in South-West Africa (now Namibia) in the late Cold War period. Perhaps unsurprisingly, given the quantity of arms and materiel supplied by the Soviet Union and the large number of KGB and military personnel for whom serving there was a highlight of their career,[46] trade and other relations with Angola recovered early when compared to other southern African states.

In addition, Russian economic activity there sees an unusual diversity. An agreement signed in June 1998 during an Angolan presidential visit to Moscow resolved the Soviet debt issue in exchange for guaranteeing Russian interests in diamond mining in Angola. At the same time, Angola placed a large arms order for aircraft and infantry fighting vehicles (IFVs). This was swiftly followed in August 1998, by an agreement on repair, maintenance, and upgrade of former Soviet military equipment in Angola, signed during an official visit by Russian Defense Minister Igor Sergeyev.[47] The deals attracted criticism that suggested they were funded by illegal diamond traffic. The Russian diamond mining company, Alrosa, which operates two mines in Angola under the 1992 investment noted in Table 2, announced expansion into the construction sector there during the June 2009 visit by President Medvedev.[48] In October 2006 Gazprom announced the investment of up to $100 million in exploration and production of oil and gas in Angola, in conjunction with Sonangol, the only state owned oil and gas exploration company.[49] In 2012, Russia was scheduled to build and launch a $25.6 million telecommunications satellite for Angola, dubbed AngoSat, however, the launch of the satellite was postponed until 2014.[50] The overall Angosat project is funded to a total of $295 million by Vneshekonombank, Roseximbank, and others.[51]

Still, despite these investment plans, by 2007 Russia was not in the top five major exporters or importers of goods from Angola.[52] In a similar manner, countries such as Namibia see Russian economic involvement as heavily concentrated in the resource sector. From 2000 to 2010, Russia was insignificant in calculations of foreign direct investment (FDI) in Namibia. Following President Medvedev's visit in 2009, Moscow pledged to invest approximately $1 billion in exploiting uranium deposits in Namibia over the subsequent 5 years.[53] The Russian delegation also expressed its readiness to construct two hydroelectric power stations. Expansion of uranium extraction tallies with Russia's strategic plans, and, as a result, the Russian-owned company SWA Uranium Mines is to receive Russian government funding to expand its operations.[54] But it should be noted that, despite declarations and promises of investment, at the time of this writing, none of the specific projects heralded during Medvedev's 2009 visit to Sub-Saharan Africa had yet been implemented.

RESOURCE INTERESTS - ENERGY

In 2009, Russia surpassed Saudi Arabia to become the world's number one exporter of oil. Russia holds the world's largest natural gas reserves.[55] Gas, petroleum, and refined oil products account for two-thirds of Russian exports.[56] Russian oil production is projected to grow by approximately 1.5-2.5 percent in the next 2 decades. However, the level of active reserves is constantly falling, while reserves that are difficult to access are rising.[57] Therefore, to implement effectively Russia's energy policy and continue to support the annual budget, Russia must secure further oil and gas reserves. Vagit Alekperov, the president of LukOil, one of Russia's leading oil companies actively engaged in Africa, has stated that "Russian-African cooperation could help in meeting the goals of Russia's energy strategy for the year 2030."[58]

Among other high-profile and high-cost Russian state projects, Russia's defense strategy and plans for military modernization depend in large part on energy revenue. Yet for Russia, energy and defense are tied together in more ways than through budget financing. Russia links energy needs together with debt and exports of military equipment to cut beneficial deals in Africa. During Putin's high-profile visit to Algeria in 2006, a $7.5 billion deal was signed for combat aircraft, missiles, and tanks, linked to the cancellation of $5 billion of Algeria's Soviet-era debt and, during the same visit, Lukoil and Gazprom secured oil and gas concessions. Meanwhile, Libya had committed to purchase $2.5 billion of Russian arms, also linked to cancellation of $4 billion of Soviet debt—a significant factor in Russian objections to the course of foreign intervention in the Libyan civil war in 2011.[59]

The attractions of Sub-Saharan African energy reserves for producers from Russia and elsewhere are clear. According to the U.S. Department of Energy Information Administration, Angola is the second-largest oil producer in Sub-Saharan Africa behind Nigeria, and recent exploration suggests that Angola's oil and natural gas reserves may be larger than initially estimated.[60] Four geological provinces along the east coast of Africa have recently been assessed for undiscovered, technically recoverable, oil, natural gas, and natural gas liquids resources as part of the U.S. Geological Survey's (USGS) World Oil and Gas Assessment. The USGS estimated mean volumes of 27.6 billion barrels of oil, 441.1 trillion cubic feet of natural gas, and 13.77 billion barrels of natural gas liquids.[61] Industry estimates of proved, probable and possible "current producible reserves" are roughly 35 billion barrels of crude oil and 151 trillion cubic feet of gas, and the USGS estimates that the Sub-Saharan region as a whole could hold 72 billion barrels of undiscovered resource potential.[62] By 2020, Sub-Saharan Africa is predicted to account for 15-20 percent of total worldwide oil imports at about 2.5 million barrels per day.[63] This is roughly one-fifth of the Middle East's undiscovered potential. Although there is little consensus over the date at which Russian oil production will peak, lower production costs in Africa are attractive for Russian energy majors for short-term commercial as well as long-term energy security considerations.

Significant investment would be required of Russia to explore, extract, and export the mostly untapped energy resources in Sub-Saharan Africa. Investment in oil and gas exploration, production, and infrastructure development for export also depends on the security and stability of the invested country. In many countries in Sub-Saharan Africa, civil wars make investing in energy exploration even more problematic, especially over questions of claims to oil and/or gas fields, such as in Angola and Sudan. Between 1985 and 1991, civil war in Sudan forced all foreign oil companies with onshore concessions to either withdraw or suspend activity.[64] In Sub-Saharan Africa, windfalls created by oil wealth have largely contributed to widespread corruption and abuse within African governments. Oil export revenues account for a large proportion of gross domestic product, for example 40 percent in Nigeria and 85 percent in Equatorial Guinea.[65] Much of this revenue is not funneled back into economies, maintaining poverty and instability in Sub-Saharan Africa, and thus creating an unstable investment environment.

This gives rise to potential concern over Russian involvement in African energy projects:

> Europe's increasing consumption of energy and dependence on oil and gas imports from Russia puts pressure on the Kremlin to seek alternative sources of energy. Africa, with its rich endowment of crude oil reserves, natural gas deposits, and other minerals, is exerting a strong attraction for Russian energy companies. . . . As Africa's comparative advantage in the scope and frequency of new discoveries is being courted by global energy consumption countries such as Russia, precautionary measures should be put in place to ensure that sustainable economic and social benefits accrue from natural resources exploitation.[66]

While a significant consideration for Western energy companies, these problems have a demonstrably smaller deterrent effect for the huge Chinese involvement in energy extraction and production. The Russian approach to the balance between pure commercial realpolitik and sensitivity to humanitarian concerns in the energy-producing host state seems yet to be coherently determined, but is likely to fall between these two poles. As explained by one U.S. analyst:

> Energy security is now being given serious attention. . . . A case in point is how Russia and China view energy security. The U.S. debate explicitly incorporates environmental objectives and implicitly endorses iso-

lationist tendencies, while the Russian and Chinese versions explicitly promote expansionist tendencies while discounting . . . environmental objectives. For Russia, energy security means 'weaponizing' energy. It is not a philosophy that aims at some future self-sufficient 'clean energy' paradise. It is a doctrine for today, which takes the world as it is, vulnerable and addicted to 'dirty energy' such as natural gas, oil, and coal, and exploits that dependence to make Russia stronger. With this cynical way of looking at the world, much akin to the way Colombian drug lords regard cocaine addicts, Russia pursues an energy security that is quite alien to what most Americans dreamily think it to be.[67]

There are other features to Russian investment bids that could prove attractive to African nations, beyond the absence of political or ideological strings or of insistence on good behavior. Practical experience may also play a role:

Russia's well-established expertise in extracting energy resources and advanced nuclear know-how presents a value-added opportunity for Africa. It is worth noting that Russia is participating in tenders for the construction of the first nuclear power plants in Egypt and Nigeria, which have significant uranium reserves. Also, Russia's own experience with the problems that plagued its energy sector during the 1990s and its ability and knowledge to restructure the sector for improved management and higher productivity, could provide a salutary lesson to be learned by African countries.[68]

At the same time, Russian investors may not be immune to the consequences of local disaffection. In 2009, The Movement for the Emancipation of the Niger Delta (MEND) carried out an attack on an oil facility and immediately afterwards issued a statement directly addressing visiting Russian President Dmitry Medvedev, warning that "this is the fate that awaits the gas pipelines you plan to invest [in] Nigeria if justice is not factored in the whole process." The attack and statement came shortly after Gazprom had secured a $2.5 billion investment deal in Nigeria, signed during the Medvedev visit.[69]

As noted above, Russia's energy doctrine is designed to be expansionist, seeking control over resources to meet energy demands. Russia also needs to export natural gas and oil in order to support the Russian economy and enhance the dependence of other states on Russian energy reserves. With Russia supplying the EU with one-third of the energy it consumes, this can give rise to immediate concern in consumer countries.[70] Given the differing approaches to, and even definitions of, energy security between Russia on the one hand and the U.S. and its Euro-Atlantic allies on the other, control of African energy resources by Russian majors should be observed closely and the long-term implications considered with as much attention as is given to similar acquisition programs by China.

TRADE

The importance of Russia as a trading partner to African countries is slight when compared to other developed countries and emerging markets. Bilateral trade between Russia and Africa reached a peak of $7.3 billion in 2008. Although this is close to a 10-fold increase from the very low trade volume of $740 million in 1994, it is not significant enough to guarantee Russian companies a bargaining edge when engaging with African countries.[71] By comparison, total U.S. trade with Africa in 2012 amounted to $93.2 billion,[72] and Chinese trade with Africa in 2012 reached $163.9 billion in the first 10 months, up 20 percent each year, according to the Chinese Ministry of Commerce.[73]

The example of South Africa as a historically strong trading partner during Soviet times is indicative. South Africa is still the leading Russian foreign trade partner in Sub-Saharan Africa. In 2010, annual bilateral trade increased by 0.5 percent to $519.1 million, but this figure masked a dramatic collapse in export trade from Russia: the volume of exports fell by 74.5 percent to $45.8 million from $195.2 million in 2009. In the first half of 2011, the most recent figures currently available, bilateral trade turnover amounted to $234 million, showing growth of 7.9 percent compared to the same period of the previous year.[74]

Despite this recovery, Russia's trade with South Africa is still significantly below the peak of their bilateral trade in 2008 of ZAR4.2 billlion[75] — and not even bearing comparison with bilateral trade between South Africa and China, which, in the same year, reached ZAR188 billion. Russia's trade with its most important African partner is, in fact, the smallest of all of the BRIC (Brazil, Russia, India, and China) countries, the notional grouping of BRIC and South Africa, to be discussed in more detail.[76]

The growth in trade between Russia and Africa after 2000 saw Russian imports of African products increasing at a slower pace than Russian exports to the continent; furthermore, these imports came overwhelmingly from a small minority of countries, with Algeria, Egypt, Morocco, Guinea, Côte d'Ivoire, and

South Africa jointly accounting for about 80 percent of total volume. Imports from Africa rose overall from $350 million in 2000 to $1.6 billion in 2009, while exports from Africa grew from $947 million to $4 billion over the same period. Both exports and imports grew gradually from 2000 to 2008, after which the impact of the world financial and economic crisis led to a slight fall. Russia has maintained a trade surplus with Africa, standing at $597 million in 2000, rising to $3.3 billion in 2008 and falling to $2.3 billion in 2009. According to a 2011 study, despite this rapid growth, Africa still accounts for only 1 percent of Russia's world trade,[77] compared to the EU, Russia's biggest trading partner, with 46.8 percent of overall trade in 2010.[78] At the time of this writing, more recent data for trade between Russia and the region did not appear to be available: it may be a symptom of its relative insignificance that Russia's Federal State Statistics Service, in its reporting of "Foreign Trade of the Russian Federation with Countries of the Far Abroad," did not see fit to include data for a single Sub-Saharan nation.[79]

Russian and African direct trade is therefore significantly underdeveloped, compared to investment in resource extraction and cooperation on the associated financing—a feature highlighted by the mismatch between investment and bilateral trade noted in the case of Angola described above. Andrei Sharonov, managing director of Troika Dialog Group, was a member of the high-profile delegation led by Medvedev during his visit in 2009. Apparently making no mention of trade finance, Sharonov said:

> Russian businesses are interested in partnership opportunities in Africa, both in terms of access to mineral resources as well as participating in power and infra-

structure projects. My trip to Nigeria, Namibia, and Angola is meant to introduce members of the Russian delegation to [South Africa's] Standard Bank and to explore opportunities for financing Russian companies' projects on these markets.[80]

The stated intention to increase Russian business and financial integration with Sub-Saharan Africa was clear; but as noted above in the cases both of infrastructure and extraction investments and of trade, at the time of writing little, if any, concrete progress has been made since then-President Medvedev's 2009 visit. This lack of performance may be linked to the Russian absorption with other regions of the world discussed in the introduction to this Paper, but the relative inactivity compared to other foreign powers in the region risks creating or reinforcing a perception of Russia as a partner who makes promises that are then not delivered.

ARMS TRADE

Russia is the second largest arms exporter globally, behind the United States. But according to the U.S. Congressional Research Service, U.S. arms exports tripled in 2011 to a total of $66.8 billion, dwarfing Russia's next-largest total of $4.8 billion.[81] Along with the United States, Russia's primary competitor in the arms market in Africa since the fall of the USSR has been China. Moscow's main customers include India, Syria, Algeria, Myanmar, Venezuela, Sudan, and many African states such as Algeria and Ethiopia. However, Russia's arms industry has been falling behind in key technologies, and it is seeking more technologically advanced partners to develop new technology and new markets for export. According to the Stockholm International Peace Research Institute (SIPRI) Arms Transfers Database, the majority of Russian arms sold to Africa during the 1990s and early 2000s were anti-tank missiles, artillery, self-propelled guns, anti-aircraft artillery, surface to air systems, helicopters, and a small number of aircraft with associated munitions.[82] Although Sub-Saharan Africa (excluding South Africa) accounted for only 1.5 percent of the volume of world imports of major arms in 2006 to 2010, this should be seen in the context of most countries in the region having no domestic arms industry and therefore depending wholly on imports.[83]

Russia stated an intention to revive substantially military cooperation and arms sales to Africa as early as 2003. Then chairman of the State Duma Committee on Defense Army General Andrei Nikolayev announced that:

> Russia has the potential to increase the amount of military-technical cooperation [i.e., provision of military equipment] with the Arab world, Latin America, and South-East Asia. Russia works very poorly on the African continent. And there is considerable potential. The delegation of the State Duma Defense Committee which recently returned from South Africa is convinced of this.

South Africa had supposedly shown great interest in Russian armored vehicles and small arms, sparking an ambitious Russian aim to supplant the United States as the leading supplier of weapons to the country.[84]

Russia has often been accused of supplying arms to African countries where internal conflict and ethnic strife end in severe human rights violations. Russia continues to supply helicopter gunships to Sudan, where they have been used to attack civilians in Darfur and Southern Kordofan—with little of the international opposition that was sparked by a repair contract for similar helicopters supplied to the Assad regime in Syria. Russia, like China, remains wary of any arms control treaty to include binding rules on international human rights, international humanitarian law, and socio-economic development. Moscow has expressed concern that these treaties could be used as tools for the West to restrict the Russian export market in order to retain export hegemony. Russian officials argue that such rules are interpreted subjectively and ideologically,[85] and Russia is thus unlikely to commit to any conventional arms control treaty that limits their current or potential export markets.

This is particularly the case following the Russian experience of losing business with a key trading partner after the change of regime in Libya. Although Libya is not a sub-Saharan nation, the example is worth considering, as it predicates the likely future Russian response to similar situations that could potentially arise in Southern Africa. Sergei V. Chemezov, the director of the Russian state company Rostekhnologia, which plays a key role in weapons exports, claimed Russia lost a potential $4 billion as a result of the UN embargo on Libya.[86] The financial setbacks were characterized as "lost opportunity costs," as open contracts for Libya had not yet been filled when Moscow approved UNSC Resolution 1970 in February 2011.[87] Russia had mostly shipped spare parts for Libya's Soviet-built weaponry, but in 2008, Russia waived Libya's Soviet-era debt in exchange for new arms contracts, suggesting that Russian arms exporters may, in fact, have felt the loss of even more potential orders. Libya was Russia's primary customer in the Middle East and North Africa, along with Algeria and Syria, before the UNSC unanimously voted to impose sanctions.[88]

Chemezov also stated Russia could lose as much as $10 billion if the UN expanded arms embargoes to other Middle Eastern or North African countries,[89] making the approval of another arms embargo that would incur arms sales losses through the UNSC unlikely. The Russian defense industry stands to lose a great deal of money from military contracts should existing regimes collapse, especially in Syria, and Moscow is likely to be highly wary of losing more arms markets elsewhere. Africa will thus continue to be of interest to Moscow's defense industry in need of new markets and revenue, and, as a result, Russia is likely to resist any possible attempts to restrict or restrain arms supplies there.

BRAZIL, RUSSIA, INDIA, CHINA, AND SOUTH AFRICA

Russia is attracted by the notion of cooperation in Africa between countries making up the BRICS (Brazil, Russia, India, China, South Africa) virtual group of nations with supposedly similar economies. Two benefits for Russia are an enhanced ability to keep a wary eye on the activities of other BRICS states in Africa and the potential creation of a cohesive block of states to counter U.S./Western influence there.

Examples of concrete achievement in cooperation between the BRICS states are few. Yet interestingly, in Africa, a Southern African company is discussing plans with Russia and potential commercial investors, including Google, for a $1.5 billion investment in subsea cable, linking 21 African countries with Russia and the remaining BRICS states.[90] The fiber optic cable is designed to make direct connections with all BRICS countries and to avoid third country dependencies. For example, the plan calls for a direct link from China to Brazil without having to connect through hubs in the West, with the explicit aim of enhancing cyber security for the participating nations by bypassing the United States.[91]

At the same time, seen from southern Africa, Russia's involvement in these nonregional groupings can sometimes appear tangential in real terms. Even the notional BRICS grouping has to compete with a number of other acronyms where Russia does not feature at all—for instance, IBSA and BASIC.[92] Equally tellingly, these nations consider the concept of a "G8 of the South"—in which, according to a South African study on regional alliances, Russian involvement would simply "muddle the picture."[93] It can therefore be argued that Russia's participation in specific activities of this regional grouping will be of limited significance for South Africa, the "S" of the group.

IMPLICATIONS FOR U.S. POLICY

As Russia's economy increasingly relies on the exploitation of natural resources, Moscow's foreign policy will continue to be more aggressive in countering other world powers, including the United States, in securing influence over resources abroad in order to control their distribution and ensure long-term state income. Following perceived Western military intervention operations in Libya in 2011, Moscow's foreign policy has grown more aggressive in countering perceived U.S. expansionism and interests around the globe. The Russian intention to counter the U.S. presence in Africa is no different. Competition for resource control and expanded political influence will continue in Northern and Western Africa, but is likely to intensify in Sub-Saharan Africa within the next 10 years.

The surge in interest and investment by larger powers in Africa has not gone unremarked by African nations, and their relative perceptions of U.S. and Russian involvement could have significant impacts as the U.S. increases involvement in Africa. This has specific implications for U.S. military cooperation with African states.

For U.S. Department of Defense (DoD) purposes, Africa's 54 countries were consolidated under a new combatant command, U.S. Africa Command (USAFRICOM), in 2007. AFRICOM now encompasses more nations than any other Pentagon regional command. General Carter Ham, former commander of AFRICOM, explained AFRICOM aims at a conference attended by representatives from African nations in June 2012. He stated that the United States is carefully expanding efforts to provide intelligence, training, and small numbers of forces to African nations in certain situations in order to help counter terrorist activities in the region. He also said that coordinated moves by several Africa-based terrorist groups to share their training, funding, and explosive device construction materials are worrisome and pose a threat to the United States and the region. He also briefly mentioned Djibouti, where the United States has a military contingent of around 2,000 troops, as well as the "small, temporary" troop presence in other nations, like Liberia, Morocco, and Cameroon. Altogether, Ham said, the United States has trained as many as 200,000 peacekeepers and enforcement personnel from about 25 different African nations.[94] Further, former U.S. Army Africa commander Major General David Hogg disclosed the Army will begin deploying over 3,000 troops to Africa at the beginning of 2013, contributing to anti-piracy operations in the Mediterranean Sea and off the Horn of Africa, as well as in the oil-rich Gulf of Guinea. U.S. interests in Africa continue to grow, and with them the footprint of AFRICOM and the interest in exploring potential future basing options. Given the scope for direct competition with Russia, Russia's presence, interests, and allegiances in sub-Saharan Africa will become a strategic policy concern for the U.S. Army, AFRICOM, the Pentagon, and U.S. policymakers.

However, opportunities exist for cooperation on Africa-related issues between the United States and Russia. Moscow shares the U.S. concern for global stability, especially in the Middle East and Africa, where instability could directly affect Russian business and resource investment. According to the AFRICOM Commander's Intent, the most important military task in Africa is to "deter or defeat al-Qaida and other violent extremist organizations operating in Africa and deny them safe haven."[95] Moscow's rising alarm over terrorist organizations' global freedom of movement and any potential encroachment of terrorist activity toward Russian borders is also a fundamental cause for concern in Russia's view of the world, including Africa. This was highlighted as a specific issue by Russian Foreign Minister Sergei Lavrov in January 2013, discussing the increased terrorist activity in the "vacuum of power" in northern Mali, as well as the increase of illegal weapons trafficking in Libya affecting the stability of the region.[96] The overlap of interests with AFRICOM's remit is clear. In some ways, there is a parallel with Russian official attitudes to the U.S. reduction in troops in Afghanistan planned for 2014: Ambivalent attitudes to the Western military presence there have coalesced into distinct concern expressed repeatedly by President Vladimir Putin and other high ranking officials over the consequences of their withdrawal, expected to include uncontained terrorist and drug trafficking activity.[97]

The creation of AFRICOM was a cause for widespread alarm among African nations — to the apparent considerable surprise of its creators.[98] AFRICOM suffers in particular from a perceived deficit of legitimacy owing to persisting post-colonial views held among leadership elites in some African states, compounded in some cases by more positive fond memories of Soviet connections among the leadership generation. In particular, many representatives of this generation will recall education provided at Patrice Lumumba University in Moscow (Friendship of Peoples University), while even lower-ranking members of former terrorist organizations will have had more experience of the USSR than of the United States.[99]

African suspicion of U.S. intentions is reinforced by the legacy of support from the USSR for anti-colonial movements — and it is easy enough, given recent interventions in Asia led by the United States and supported by a range of European former imperial powers, to read the United States as a neo-colonialist actor. As noted in one U.S. study,

> sensing that the main purpose for AFRICOM was to increase control over — or even seize — critical resources including oil and minerals, Africans. . . . worried that the US would intervene unilaterally. . . . Overwhelmingly negative perceptions of American intent were rooted in the past and reinforced by current events.[100]

The view from African capitals is not the same as the view from the Pentagon, and it is not axiomatic that U.S. military presence is preferable for African states to that of Russia and China. Declaratory policy on the objectives and rationale for AFRICOM, as well as planning for future development of the command, should therefore remain sensitive to these perceptions and to the attraction — historical or otherwise — of Russia as an alternative.

Even after the colonial period and the Cold War, not all U.S. involvement in the continent has fostered a positive attitude to potential military involvement:

> inconsistent levels of foreign assistance undermined US credibility, especially in southern Africa. . . . Perhaps this dissatisfaction explains why SADC members expressed such hostility toward AFRICOM.[101]

At the same time, South Africa, the founding country of SADC, maintains a close and continuing relationship with Russia through a steady history of bilateral agreements, and their relationship, in combination with those of several other sub-Saharan countries such as Angola and Namibia, likely contributes heavily to these perceptions.

Although Russia's trade and investment footprint in Africa is not as widespread as that of China, Moscow is determined to expand its presence and influence in Sub-Saharan Africa, especially in cultivating mineral resources and retaining control over sources of gas and oil. Gazprom's interests in the planned Trans-Saharan gas pipeline and Russian involvement in the Angolan oil sector carry potential implications for the energy security of the United States and its European allies, particularly in the context of security of supply. Russian interests in uranium mining may also have strategic implications, as U.S. foreign policy continues to prioritize nonproliferation of nuclear materials.

U.S. actions will also be a driver for the shape of Russian involvement in Africa. As U.S. interests and presence in Africa expand, Moscow will likely respond with an even more assertive policy toward increasing its presence and influence in Africa to counter the perceived threat of U.S. expansionism. Activities by the United States and NATO, which appear innocent from a Euro-Atlantic perspective, can be perceived as deeply troubling and even threatening when viewed from Moscow, especially when they involve an extension of NATO's reach and influence. In 2012, NATO's former Allied Commander Europe (SACEUR), U.S. Navy Admiral James Stavridis, spoke of expanding NATO cooperation around the world, including for the first time "exploring possibilities with . . . India and Brazil," two BRICS countries. He also recommended Libya as a candidate for NATO's Mediterranean Dialogue military partnership, an organization that includes every North African nation, Egypt, Tunisia, Morocco, and Algeria, except Libya. Stavridis stated in June 2012:

> Today, the Mediterranean Dialogue, we're in the process of talking, for example, with Libya. Already many of the other nations in General Ham's [AFRICOM's] region are part of this. The nations around the Mediterranean are natural NATO partners.[102]

Expansion or enhancement of U.S. involvement with African states, especially if they carry a military dimension as through AFRICOM or NATO, can be expected to provoke a defensive response from Russia, and this potential response should be considered carefully in order to reduce the transactional cost of Russian opposition or obstructionism.

Overall, the United States has rather unsuccessfully courted sub-Saharan Africa as a strategic partner. Countries such as Angola are an important source of U.S. oil imports, and sub-Saharan Africa's collective economic growth trajectory makes it a potentially powerful and influential continental player. But ambivalent memories of previous U.S. involvement and the already strong relationships with China and growing relationships with Russia, neither of which presses governments on issues of corruption, human rights, or democracy, has caused U.S. efforts to receive a welcome in some sub-Saharan countries that is lukewarm at best.[103] U.S. policy will be most successful through prioritizing interests and consistently heavily investing in top priority areas in order to gain the trust not only of the governments currently in power, but also, and more importantly, of the next generations of leaders in these nations. Sub-Saharan Africa needs and is looking for a dependable ally, not just the highest bidder investor; the highest bid and the greatest investment are currently winning the greatest influence, but do not guarantee long-term allegiance. U.S. policy still has a foothold to ensure an operable environment for the growing U.S. presence in Africa, should it choose to use it.

OUTLOOK

At the time of writing, Russian foreign policy is preoccupied with a number of immediate concerns, including the aftermath of the Arab Spring in the Middle East, the conflict in Syria, relations with Europe and NATO, especially in finding a compromise on European missile defense, and investing considerable soft power capital in the near abroad. Little obvious attention has therefore been devoted lately to sub-Saharan Africa in high-level public diplomacy. However, while Africa may not be an immediate policy priority, at a longer-term strategic level, the desire remains for Moscow to establish and maintain a more clear and defined presence in the region. Russia's dependency on natural resources to maintain its state budget and ensure future reserves for its export-based economy will ensure Moscow's continued interest in sub-Saharan Africa, and a visible return to prominence on the list of Russia's foreign policy priorities should be expected.

ENDNOTES

1. Sergius Yakobson, "Russia and Africa," *The Slavonic and East European Review*, Vol. 17, No. 51, April 1939, p. 623.

2. "Bulging in the Middle," *The Economist*, October 20, 2012.

3. Jeremy Bervoets, "The Soviet Union in Angola: Soviet and African Perspectives on the Failed Socialist Transformation," *Vestnik, The Journal Of Russian And Asian Studies*, May 11, 2011, available from *www.sras.org/the_soviet_union_in_angola*.

4. *Ibid.*

5. Sam Nolutshungu, "Soviet Involvement in Southern Africa," *Annals of the American Academy of Political and Social Science*, Vol. 481, No. 1, September 1985, pp. 138-146, 142.

6. Personal conversations with author. For a detailed overview of Soviet military and KGB presence and interventions in the region, see Vladimir Shubin, *The Hot Cold War — The USSR In Southern Africa*, Scottsville, South Africa: University of KwaZulu-Natal Press, 2008, dedicated to "one of the unsung Soviet heroes."

7. An event not publicized either in Ghana or the USSR at the time, since neither wished to avow the close relationship between Nkrumah and his KGB advisors or mentors. See, for example, John Barron, *KGB*, New York: Bantam, 1974.

8. Roger Faligot and Rémi Kauffer, *KGB Objectif Pretoria*, Paris, France: Favre, 1986, p. 134.

9. Vladimir Shubin, *ANC – A View From Moscow*, Auckland Park, South Africa: Jacana, 2008, p. ix.

10. Ivetta Gerasimchuk, "Re-Think Russian Investment in Southern Africa," *WWF's Trade and Investment Programme Report*, Moscow, Russia/Johannesburg, South Africa: WWF, 2009, p. 32, available from *mpra.ub.uni-muenchen.de/15151/*.

11. Reginald Brope, "The $56 Billion Dollar Man: Igor Sechin," forthcoming May 2013.

12. Roger Faligot and Rémi Kauffer, *KGB Objectif Pretoria*, Paris, France: Favre, 1986, pp. 101-104.

13. *Ibid.*, pp. 30-41.

14. See, for instance, Shubin, *ANC – A View From Moscow*, p. x.

15. *The Mitrokhin Archive II – The KGB And The World*, London, UK: Allen Lane, 2005.

16. Igho Natufe, "A Review of Russia-Africa Relations: New Challenges and Opportunities," August 11, 2011, available from *myafrica.ru/en/?p=439*.

17. Gregory Chin and Anton Malkin, "Russia as a Re-Emerging Donor: Catching Up in Africa," March 8, 2012, available from *www.cigionline.org/publications/2012/3/russia-re-emerging-donor-catching-up-africa*.

18. Shubin, *ANC – A View From Moscow*, p. 314.

19. *Ibid.*, pp. 317-318.

20. Natufe.

21. *Vneshnaya politika Rossii: Otnosheniya Rossii so stranami Afriki k Yugu ot Sakhary* (*Russian Foreign Policy: Relations Between Russia and Sub-Saharan Africa, Russian Federation Ministry of Foreign Affairs*), December 31, 2006, available from *rus.rusemb.at/ aussenpolitik/202.*

22. Gerasimchuk, p. 33.

23. Habiba Ben Barka and Kupukile Mlambo, "Russia's Economic Engagement with Africa," *Africa Economic Brief*, Vol. 2, Issue 7, May 11, 2011.

24. Kester Kenn Klomegah, "Russia and Africa: Economic Diplomacy Needs New Strategies," *Russia Beyond The Headlines*, August 17, 2011, p.2, available from *rbth.ru/articles/2011/08/ 17/russia_and_africa_economic_diplomacy_needs_new_strategies_ 13260.html.*

25. *Obmen dollarov na vliyaniye i resursy: kitaytsy v Afrike* (*Exchanging dollars for influence and resources: the Chinese in Africa*), Geneva, Switzerland: International Centre for Sustainable Trade and Development, December 2009, available from *ictsd.org/i/news%20 /%20bridgesrussian/65199/.*

26. Tatyana Deych, "*Kitay zavoyovyvayet Afriku*" ("China is conquering Africa"), Moscow, Russia: Russian Council for International Affairs, June 26, 2012, available from *russiancouncil.ru/ inner/?id_4=547.*

27. Natufe.

28. Shubin, *ANC – A View From Moscow*, p. 5.

29. According to Konstantin Kosachev, speaking at a conference of ambassadors and permanent representatives of the Russian Federation, July 11, 2012, available from *interaffairs.ru/read. php?item=8606.*

30. Claire Provost, "The Rebirth of Russian Foreign Aid," *The Guardian*, May 25, 2011, available from *www.guardian.co.uk/global-development/2011/may/25/russia-foreign-aid-report-influence-image*.

31. Alex Anishyuk, "Government Raises Foreign Aid 4-Fold," *St. Petersburg Times*, February 19, 2010.

32. "Peter Fradkov Shares His Views About the Current Russian-African Relations," *Russia-Africa Partnership and Success*, undated interview, available from *rusafr.com/index.php?option=com_content&view=article&id=203*.

33. Daniel Nawsaw, "China and Russia Veto Zimbabwe Sanctions," *The Guardian*, July 11, 2008, available from *www.guardian.co.uk/world/2008/jul/11/unitednations.zimbabwe*.

34. "Margelov to Meet African Leaders to Discuss 'Arab Spring', Political Situation," Interfax, August 27, 2012; "On the working trip of Deputy Minister of Foreign Affairs of Russia M. L. Bogdanov to Zimbabwe," Ministry of Foreign Affairs of the Russian Federation, August 22, 2012.

35. "Les soutiens du médiateur russe dans le conflit libyen" ("The Concerns of the Russian Mediator in the Libyan Conflict"), *Le monde du renseignement* blog, June 21, 2011, available from *lemondedurenseignement.hautetfort.com/archive/2011/06/21/les-soutiens-de-mikhail-margelov.html*.

36. Vladimir Shubin, "Russia and Africa: Coming Back?" *Russian Analytical Digest*, No. 83, Septembeer 24, 2010, p. 6.

37. "UN Mission's Summary detailed by Country," available from *www.un.org/en/peacekeeping/contributors/2012/august12_3.pdf*.

38. "Russia-African Union ties have great potential - Lavrov," *Voice of Russia*, October 21, 2011, available from *english.ruvr.ru/2011/10/21/59136129.html*.

39. *Ibid.*

40. "About the Ministry of Economic Development of the Russian Federation," in Russian, available from *www.economy. gov.ru/minec/about/structure/depAsiaAfrica/*.

41. "Foreign Economic Strategy of the Russian Federation to 2020," December 2008, in Russian, available from *www.economy. gov.ru/minec/activity/sections/foreigneconomicactivity/vec2020*.

42. Gerasimchuk, p. 32.

43. SADC includes Angola, Botswana, Democratic Republic of Congo, DRC, Lesotho, Madagascar, Malawi, Mauritius, Mozambique, Namibia, Seychelles, South Africa, Swaziland, United Republic of Tanzania, Zambia, and Zimbabwe. See *www.sadc.int*.

44. Table extracted from Gerasimchuk, p. 31.

45. Habiba Ben Barka, "Russia's Economic Engagement with Africa," *Africa Economic Brief*, Vol. 2, Issue 7, May 11, 2011.

46. See also discussion in Brope, "Sechin."

47. *Voyenno-tekhnicheskoye sotrudnichestvo s almazodobyvayush-chimi stranami Afriki (Military-Technical Cooperation with Diamond Extracting Countries of Africa)*, Moscow, Russia: Civil Centre for Applied Research, September 2005, available from *www.civilre-search.ru/pdf/10.pdf*.

48. "Alrosa to Invest $500 mln in Angola Building Sector," *Reuters*, August 19, 2009, available from *www.reuters.com/ article/2009/08/19/angola-russia-alrosa-idUSB61034520090819*.

49. "Gazprom to Invest $100 mln in Angola Oil & Gas Projects," *RIA Novosti*, October 31, 2006, available from *en.rian.ru/rus-sia/20061031/55268264.html*.

50. "Launch of Angola's First Satellite Postponed until 2014," *Macauhub*, Macau, November 30, 2012, available from *www.ma-cauhub.com.mo/en/2012/11/30/launch-of-angolas-first-satellite-post-poned-until-2014/*.

51. "Angola to Spend U.S.$25.6 Million in 2011 to Begin Construction of Angosat Satellite," *Macauhub*, Macau, March 18, 2011, available from *www.macauhub.com.mo/en/2011/03/18/angola-to-spend-us25-6-million-in-2011-to-begin-construction-of-angosat-satellite/*.

52. Hamet Aguemon, Isaac Mireles, and Shelly Ogilvie, "Angola Financial Systems," undated, available from *fic.wharton. upenn.edu/fic/africa/angola%20final-final.pdf*.

53. "Russia to Invest $1 bln in Namibia Uranium Deposits," *RIA Novosti*, May 20, 2010, available from *en.rian.ru/ world/20100520/159091599.html*.

54. Fantu Cheru, "NAI to Initiate Research on BRIC-Africa Relations; Russia's New Resource Diplomacy in Africa," *Nordiska Afrikainstitutet*, undated, available from *www.nai.uu.se/Report-BRICsSummitMoscow.pdf*.

55. Energy Info Admin, "Russia Energy Profile," *Petroleum*, Washington, DC: U.S. Departmentt of Energy, September 16, 2009.

56. Olga Oliker, Keith Crane, Lowell H. Schwartz, and Catherin Yusupov, *Russian Foreign Policy: Sources and Implications*, Santa Monica, CA: RAND Corporation, April 1, 2009, p. 52.

57. Dmitry Mikhailov, "Key Elements of Oil Production," *Oil of Russia*, Vol. 39, No. 2, 2009, available from *www.oilru.com/ or/39/784*.

58. Natufe.

59. Vivienne Watt, "Russia Rearms," *Time*, April 27, 2009, available from *www.time.com/time/printout/0,8816,1891681,00.html*.

60. "Country Analysis Brief; Angola," Washington, DC: U.S. Energy Information Administration, October 16, 2012, available at *www.eia.gov/countries/country-data.cfm?fips=AO*.

61. "Assessment of Undiscovered Oil and Gas Resources of Four East Africa Geologic Provinces," World Petroleum Resourc-

es Project, New Cumberland, PA: U.S. Geological Survey, April 2012, available from *pubs.usgs.gov/fs/2012/3039/*.

62. T. Hemsted, "Second and Third Millennium Reserves Development in African Basins," T. Arthur, D. S. MacGregor, and N. R. Cameron, eds., *Petroleum Geology of Africa: New Themes and Developing Technologies*, London, UK: Geological Society, 2003, p. 241.

63. *Ibid.*

64. Paul F Hueper, "Sub-Saharan Africa," David L. David and Jan H. Kalicki, eds., *Energy and Security: Toward a New Foreign Policy Strategy*, Baltimore, PA: John Hopkins University Press, 2005, p. 251.

65. *Ibid.*, p. 249.

66. Barka and Mlambo.

67. Article by Michael Frodl, National Defense Industrial Association (NDIA), *Business and Technology Magazine*, cited in Oliker *et al.*, p. 52.

68. Barka and Mlambo.

69. "After Shell pipeline blast in Nigeria, MEND threatens Russia," Montreal, Canada: Global Research, Center for Research on Globalization, June 25, 2009, available from *www.globalresearch. ca/after-shell-pipeline-blast-in-nigeria-mend-threatens-russia/*.

70. See, for example, Luke Harding and David Hearst. "Europe Fears Winter Energy Crisis as Russia Tightens Grip on Oil Supplies," *The Observer*, September 13, 2009, available from *www. guardian.co.uk/world/2009/sep/13/russia-oil-exports-eu/print*.

71. Barka and Mlambo.

72. United States Census Bureau, "2012: US Trade in Goods with Africa," *Foreign Trade*, Washington, DC: U.S. Department of Trade, available from *www.census.gov/foreign-trade/balance/ c0013.html*.

73. "China-Africa Trade Likely to Hit Record High," Forum on China Africa Cooperation, December 28, 2012, available from *www.focac.org/eng/zfgx/jmhz/t1001387.htm*.

74. "Russian-South African Economic Cooperation," available from *www.russianembassy.org.za/economic/Coop.html*.

75. Quoted in South African Rand, since wide fluctuations in the exchange rate with the U.S. dollar make direct comparisons with the dollar figures cited previously unhelpful.

76. "Steady Growth in SA Trade With BRICS Members," South African Government News Agency, August 29, 2012.

77. Barka and Mlambo.

78. "Russia Trade, Exports and Imports," *EconomyWatch*, March 17, 2010, available from *www.economywatch.com/world_economy/russia/export-import.html*.

79. "*Vneshnyaya torgovlya Rossiyskoy Federatsii so stranami dal'nego zarubezh'ya*" ("Foreign Trade of the Russian Federation with Countries of the Far Abroad"), available from *www.gks.ru/wps/wcm/connect/rosstat/rosstatsite/main/trade/*.

80. "Stanbic Partners With Russian Investment Group," *Buziness Africa*, October 6, 2009, available from *www.buzinessafrica.com/index.php?option=com_content&view=article&id=232:stanbic-partners-with-russian-investment-group&catid=5:investment&Itemid=7&lang=fr*.

81. "Do We Have Statistics on China's Africa 'Land Grab'?" *China in Africa, The Real Story*, August 30, 2010, available from *www.chinaafricarealstory.com/2010/08/do-we-have-statistics-on-chinas-africa.html*.

82. SIPRI Arms Transfers Database, available from *www.sipri.org/databases/armstransfers*.

83. Pieter D; Wezeman, T. Siemon, Lucie Béraud-Sudreau, *Arms Flow to Sub-Saharan Africa*, Stockholm, Sweden: SIPRI, December 2011, available from *books.sipri.org/files/PP/SIPRIPP30.pdf*.

84. *"Novosti VPK i voyenno-tekhnicheskogo sotrudnichestva"* ("Military Industrial Complex and Military-Technical Cooperation News"), *Military Industrial Complex and Military-Technical Cooperation News*, July 19-25, 2003, available from *mfit.ru/defensive/obzor/ob25-07-03-1.html*.

85. "The 'Big Six' Arms Exporters," *Amnesty International*, June 11, 2012, available from *www.amnesty.org/en/news/big-six-arms-exporters-2012-06-11*.

86. Andrew E. Kramer, "Unrest in Libya and the Middle East Is Costing the Russian Arms Industry," *New York Times*, March 4, 2011, available from *www.nytimes.com/2011/03/05/world/europe/05russia.html?_r=1*.

87. "Security Council Imposes Sanctions on Libyan Authorities in Bid to Stem Violent Repression," *UN News Center*, February 26, 2011, available from *www.un.org/apps/news/story.asp?NewsID=37633#.UEyNTiJTYTA*.

88. "Russian Arms Sales to the Middle East and North Africa," February 17th Libyan Youth Movement, July 4, 2011, available from *feb17.info/news/russian-arms-sales-to-the-middle-east-and-north-africa/*.

89. Andrew E. Kramer, "Unrest in Libya and the Middle East Is Costing the Russian Arms Industry," *New York Times*, March 4, 2011, available from *www.nytimes.com/2011/03/05/world/europe/05russia.html?_r=1*.

90. "Braziliyu, Rossiyu, Indiyu, Kitay, Afriku i SShA soyedinyet magistralyu" ("Brazil, Russia, India, China, Africa and USA To Be Linked by Main Line"), *Telekomza*, June 5, 2012, available from *telekomza.ru/2012/06/05/braziliyu-rossiyu-indiyu-kitaj-afriku-i-ssha-soedinyat-magistralyu/*. See also "Investors Mull $1.5 billion BRICS Undersea Cable," *IT Web Africa*, June 5, 2012, available from *www.itwebafrica.com/internet/334-africa/229374-investors-mull-15bn-brics-undersea-cable*.

91. Tom Espiner, "i3 Africa Calls for BRICS Submarine Cable Cash" *Security Bulletin*, April 17, 2012, available from *www.zdnet.com/i3-africa-calls-for-brics-submarine-cable-cash-4010025904/*.

92. India, Brazil, South Africa; and Brazil, Brazil, South Africa, India, China.

93. "From BRIC To BRICS: Report On The Proceedings Of The International Workshop On South Africa's Emerging Power Alliances: IBSA, BRICS, BASIC," Johannesburg, South Africa, Institute for Global Dialogue, 2011.

94. Boris Volkhonsky, *U.S. Military Expansion in Africa Aimed at China*, Montreal, Canada: Global Research: Center for Research on Globalization, June 28, 2012, available from *www.globalresearch.ca/u-s-military-expansion-in-africa-aimed-at-china/*.

95. Available from *www.africom.mil/what-we-do*.

96. "Moscow Concerned over Mali Terror Surge," *Voice of Russia*, January 14, 2013, available from *english.ruvr.ru/2013_01_14/Moscow-concerned-over-Mali-terror-surge/*.

97. "Putin Reiterates Support for NATO Afghan Operation," *Ria Novosti*, August 1, 2012, available from *en.rian.ru/russia/20120801/174911173.html*.

98. El-Rayah A. Osman, "More Than Good Intentions: AFRICOM, between American Ambition and African Suspicion," *Military Intelligence Professional Bulletin*, January-March 2012, pp. 21-26.

99. Resulting not only from extensive military training programs in the USSR, but also from unplanned events like the mass evacuation of Umkhonto we Sizwe from Tanzania to the USSR in 1969. See Shubin, *ANC - A View From Moscow*, p. 78.

100. Diana B Putnam, "Addressing African Questions About the Legitimacy of the U.S. Africa Command, AFRICOM," in Amy Krakowka and Laurel Hummel, eds., *Understanding Africa — A Geographic Approach*, West Point, NY: United States Military Academy, 2009, pp. 128-129.

101. *Ibid.*, p. 131.

102. Rick Rozoff, *Libya: New AFRICOM and NATO Beachhead in Africa*, Montreal, Canada: Global Research: Center for Research on Globalization, June 17, 2012, available from *www.globalresearch.ca/libya-new-africom-and-nato-beachhead-in-africa/*.

103. Jennifer G. Cooke, "Angola's Elections: Watershed Moment or More of the Same?" Washington, DC: Center for Strategic and International Studies, August 31, 2012, available from *csis.org/publication/angolas-elections-watershed-moment-or-more-same*.

www.ingramcontent.com/pod-product-compliance
Lightning Source LLC
Chambersburg PA
CBHW070500290526
45790CB00003B/1031